MY LITTLE QUOTEBOOK

Because every quote tells a story...

When was it said? _____

Where? _____

"

"

How would you describe it?

Funny ☐   Profound ☐   Silly ☐   Bizarre ☐

Age? _____

When was it said? _____ Age?

Where? _____

"

Funny ☐   Profound ☐   Silly ☐   Bizarre ☐

When was it said? _____ Age?

Where? _____

"

Funny ☐   Profound ☐   Silly ☐   Bizarre ☐

When was it said? _____

Where? _____

"

"

How would you describe it?

Funny ☐   Profound ☐   Silly ☐   Bizarre ☐

Age? _____

When was it said? _____ Age?

Where? _____

"

Funny ☐ Profound ☐ Silly ☐ Bizarre ☐

"

When was it said? _____ Age?

Where? _____

"

Funny ☐ Profound ☐ Silly ☐ Bizarre ☐

"

When was it said? _____

Where? _____

How would you describe it?

Funny ☐   Profound ☐   Silly ☐   Bizarre ☐

Age? _____

When was it said? _____ Age? _____

Where? _____

"

Funny ☐   Profound ☐   Silly ☐   Bizarre ☐

When was it said? _____ Age? _____

Where? _____

"

Funny ☐   Profound ☐   Silly ☐   Bizarre ☐

When was it said? _____

Where? _____

How would you describe it?

Funny ☐　　Profound ☐　　Silly ☐　　Bizarre ☐

Age? [　　　　　　　]

When was it said? _____ Age? [   ]

Where? _____

" "

Funny ☐   Profound ☐   Silly ☐   Bizarre ☐

When was it said? _____ Age? [   ]

Where? _____

" "

Funny ☐   Profound ☐   Silly ☐   Bizarre ☐

When was it said? _____

Where? _____

How would you describe it?

Funny ☐ Profound ☐ Silly ☐ Bizarre ☐

Age? _____

When was it said? _____ Age? ____

Where? _____

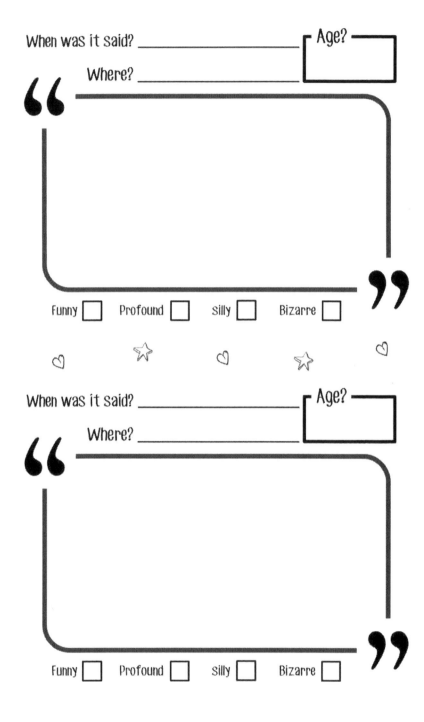

Funny ☐   Profound ☐   Silly ☐   Bizarre ☐

When was it said? _____ Age? ____

Where? _____

Funny ☐   Profound ☐   Silly ☐   Bizarre ☐

When was it said? _____

Where? _____

"

"

How would you describe it?

Funny ☐   Profound ☐   Silly ☐   Bizarre ☐

Age? ☐

When was it said? _____ Age? _____

Where? _____

"

Funny ☐   Profound ☐   Silly ☐   Bizarre ☐

"

When was it said? _____ Age? _____

Where? _____

"

Funny ☐   Profound ☐   Silly ☐   Bizarre ☐

"

When was it said? _____

Where? _____

,"

How would you describe it?

Funny ☐   Profound ☐   silly ☐   Bizarre ☐

Age? ☐

When was it said? _____ Age?

Where? _____

"

Funny ☐   Profound ☐   Silly ☐   Bizarre ☐

When was it said? _____ Age?

Where? _____

"

Funny ☐   Profound ☐   Silly ☐   Bizarre ☐

When was it said? _____

Where? _____

"

"

How would you describe it?

Funny ☐ Profound ☐ Silly ☐ Bizarre ☐

Age? _____

When was it said? _____ Age? _____

Where? _____

"

Funny ☐   Profound ☐   silly ☐   Bizarre ☐

When was it said? _____ Age? _____

Where? _____

"

Funny ☐   Profound ☐   silly ☐   Bizarre ☐

When was it said? _____

Where? _____

"

"

How would you describe it?

Funny ☐　　Profound ☐　　Silly ☐　　Bizarre ☐

Age? ☐

When was it said? _____ Age? _____

Where? _____

"

Funny ☐   Profound ☐   Silly ☐   Bizarre ☐

When was it said? _____ Age? _____

Where? _____

"

Funny ☐   Profound ☐   Silly ☐   Bizarre ☐

When was it said? _____

Where? _____

"

How would you describe it?

Funny ☐   Profound ☐   Silly ☐   Bizarre ☐

Age? ☐

When was it said? _____ Age?

Where? _____

"

"

Funny ☐   Profound ☐   Silly ☐   Bizarre ☐

When was it said? _____ Age?

Where? _____

"

"

Funny ☐   Profound ☐   Silly ☐   Bizarre ☐

When was it said? _____

Where? _____

"

"

How would you describe it?

Funny ☐   Profound ☐   Silly ☐   Bizarre ☐

Age? [ ]

When was it said? _____ Age? _____

Where? _____

"

Funny ☐   Profound ☐   Silly ☐   Bizarre ☐

When was it said? _____ Age? _____

Where? _____

"

Funny ☐   Profound ☐   Silly ☐   Bizarre ☐

When was it said? _____

Where? _____

How would you describe it?

Funny ☐   Profound ☐   Silly ☐   Bizarre ☐

Age? _____

When was it said? _____ Age? _____

Where? _____

"

Funny ☐   Profound ☐   Silly ☐   Bizarre ☐

When was it said? _____ Age? _____

Where? _____

"

Funny ☐   Profound ☐   Silly ☐   Bizarre ☐

When was it said? _____

Where? _____

"

How would you describe it?

Funny ☐   Profound ☐   Silly ☐   Bizarre ☐

Age? ☐

☆   ☆

When was it said? _____ Age?

Where? _____

"

Funny ☐ Profound ☐ Silly ☐ Bizarre ☐

When was it said? _____ Age?

Where? _____

"

Funny ☐ Profound ☐ Silly ☐ Bizarre ☐

When was it said? _____

Where? _____

"

How would you describe it?

Funny ☐   Profound ☐   Silly ☐   Bizarre ☐

Age? _____

When was it said? _____ Age? _____

Where? _____

"

Funny ☐   Profound ☐   Silly ☐   Bizarre ☐

When was it said? _____ Age? _____

Where? _____

"

Funny ☐   Profound ☐   Silly ☐   Bizarre ☐

When was it said? _____

Where? _____

"

"

How would you describe it?

Funny ☐   Profound ☐   Silly ☐   Bizarre ☐

Age? _____

When was it said? _____ Age?

Where? _____

"

"

Funny ☐ Profound ☐ Silly ☐ Bizarre ☐

When was it said? _____ Age?

Where? _____

"

"

Funny ☐ Profound ☐ Silly ☐ Bizarre ☐

When was it said? _____

Where? _____

"

"

How would you describe it?

Funny ☐   Profound ☐   Silly ☐   Bizarre ☐

Age? _____

When was it said? _____ Age?

"

Where? _____

Funny ☐ Profound ☐ Silly ☐ Bizarre ☐

"

When was it said? _____ Age?

"

Where? _____

Funny ☐ Profound ☐ Silly ☐ Bizarre ☐

"

When was it said? _____

Where? _____

" "

How would you describe it?

Funny ☐   Profound ☐   Silly ☐   Bizarre ☐

Age? ⎍

When was it said? _____ Age?

Where? _____

"

Funny ☐   Profound ☐   Silly ☐   Bizarre ☐

When was it said? _____ Age?

Where? _____

"

Funny ☐   Profound ☐   Silly ☐   Bizarre ☐

When was it said? _____

Where? _____

How would you describe it?

Funny ☐   Profound ☐   Silly ☐   Bizarre ☐

Age? _____

When was it said? _____ Age? ____

Where? _____

"

Funny ☐   Profound ☐   Silly ☐   Bizarre ☐

"

When was it said? _____ Age? ____

Where? _____

"

Funny ☐   Profound ☐   Silly ☐   Bizarre ☐

"

When was it said? _____

Where? _____

"

How would you describe it?

Funny ☐   Profound ☐   Silly ☐   Bizarre ☐

Age? _____

When was it said? _____ Age?

Where? _____

" "

Funny ☐ Profound ☐ Silly ☐ Bizarre ☐

When was it said? _____ Age?

Where? _____

" "

Funny ☐ Profound ☐ Silly ☐ Bizarre ☐

When was it said? _____

Where? _____

How would you describe it?

Funny ☐   Profound ☐   Silly ☐   Bizarre ☐

Age? _____

When was it said? _____ Age? _____

Where? _____

" "

Funny ☐   Profound ☐   Silly ☐   Bizarre ☐

When was it said? _____ Age? _____

Where? _____

" "

Funny ☐   Profound ☐   Silly ☐   Bizarre ☐

When was it said? _____

Where? _____

" "

How would you describe it?

Funny ☐   Profound ☐   Silly ☐   Bizarre ☐

Age? _____

When was it said? _____ ⌐ Age? ___⌐

Where? _____

"

Funny ☐   Profound ☐   Silly ☐   Bizarre ☐

When was it said? _____ ⌐ Age? ___⌐

Where? _____

"

Funny ☐   Profound ☐   Silly ☐   Bizarre ☐

When was it said? _____

Where? _____

"

How would you describe it?

Funny ☐   Profound ☐   Silly ☐   Bizarre ☐

Age? _____

When was it said? _____ Age? _____

Where? _____

"

Funny ☐   Profound ☐   Silly ☐   Bizarre ☐

When was it said? _____ Age? _____

Where? _____

"

Funny ☐   Profound ☐   Silly ☐   Bizarre ☐

When was it said? _____

Where? _____

How would you describe it?

Funny ☐   Profound ☐   Silly ☐   Bizarre ☐

Age? _____

When was it said? _____ **Age?** _____

Where? _____

" "

Funny ☐   Profound ☐   Silly ☐   Bizarre ☐

When was it said? _____ **Age?** _____

Where? _____

" "

Funny ☐   Profound ☐   Silly ☐   Bizarre ☐

When was it said? _____

Where? _____

How would you describe it?

Funny ☐   Profound ☐   Silly ☐   Bizarre ☐

Age? _____

When was it said? _____ Age? [   ]

Where? _____

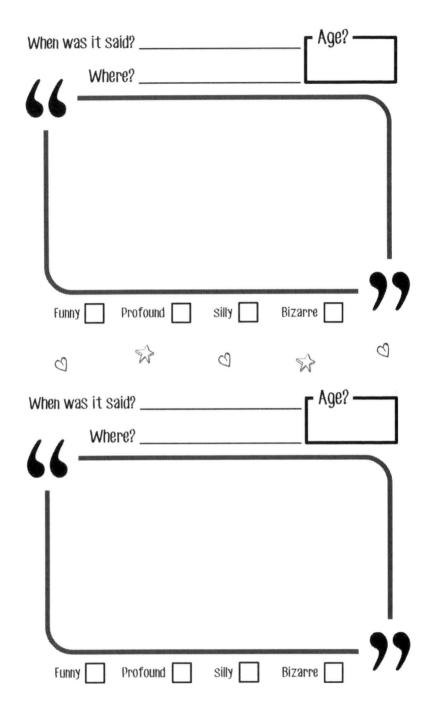

Funny [ ]   Profound [ ]   Silly [ ]   Bizarre [ ]

When was it said? _____ Age? [   ]

Where? _____

Funny [ ]   Profound [ ]   Silly [ ]   Bizarre [ ]

When was it said? _____

Where? _____

How would you describe it?

Funny ☐   Profound ☐   Silly ☐   Bizarre ☐

Age? _____

When was it said? _____ Age? _____

Where? _____

"

Funny ☐   Profound ☐   silly ☐   Bizarre ☐

When was it said? _____ Age? _____

Where? _____

"

Funny ☐   Profound ☐   silly ☐   Bizarre ☐

When was it said? _____

Where? _____

"

How would you describe it?

Funny ☐   Profound ☐   Silly ☐   Bizarre ☐

Age? _____

When was it said? _____ Age?

Where? _____

"

Funny ☐   Profound ☐   Silly ☐   Bizarre ☐

When was it said? _____ Age?

Where? _____

"

Funny ☐   Profound ☐   Silly ☐   Bizarre ☐

When was it said? _____

Where? _____

How would you describe it?

Funny ☐   Profound ☐   Silly ☐   Bizarre ☐

Age? ☐

When was it said? _____ Age?

Where? _____

"

Funny ☐   Profound ☐   Silly ☐   Bizarre ☐

"

When was it said? _____ Age?

Where? _____

"

Funny ☐   Profound ☐   Silly ☐   Bizarre ☐

"

When was it said? _____

Where? _____

How would you describe it?

Funny ☐   Profound ☐   Silly ☐   Bizarre ☐

Age? _____

When was it said? _____ Age?

Where? _____

"

Funny ☐   Profound ☐   Silly ☐   Bizarre ☐

When was it said? _____ Age?

Where? _____

"

Funny ☐   Profound ☐   Silly ☐   Bizarre ☐

When was it said? _____

Where? _____

"

"

How would you describe it?

Funny ☐   Profound ☐   Silly ☐   Bizarre ☐

Age? ☐

When was it said? _____ Age? _____

Where? _____

"

Funny ☐   Profound ☐   Silly ☐   Bizarre ☐

"

When was it said? _____ Age? _____

Where? _____

"

Funny ☐   Profound ☐   Silly ☐   Bizarre ☐

"

When was it said? _____

Where? _____

"

How would you describe it?

Funny ☐   Profound ☐   Silly ☐   Bizarre ☐

Age? _____

When was it said? _____ Age? [ ]

Where? _____

"

Funny [ ]   Profound [ ]   Silly [ ]   Bizarre [ ]

When was it said? _____ Age? [ ]

Where? _____

"

Funny [ ]   Profound [ ]   Silly [ ]   Bizarre [ ]

When was it said? _____

Where? _____

How would you describe it?

Funny ☐   Profound ☐   Silly ☐   Bizarre ☐

Age? _____

When was it said? _____ Age?

Where? _____

"

Funny ☐ Profound ☐ Silly ☐ Bizarre ☐

When was it said? _____ Age?

Where? _____

"

Funny ☐ Profound ☐ Silly ☐ Bizarre ☐

When was it said? _____

Where? _____

"

"

How would you describe it?

Funny ☐   Profound ☐   Silly ☐   Bizarre ☐

Age? _____

When was it said? _____ Age? _____

Where? _____

"

Funny ☐   Profound ☐   Silly ☐   Bizarre ☐

"

When was it said? _____ Age? _____

Where? _____

"

Funny ☐   Profound ☐   Silly ☐   Bizarre ☐

"

When was it said? _____

Where? _____

"

How would you describe it?

Funny ☐   Profound ☐   Silly ☐   Bizarre ☐

Age? ☐

When was it said? _____ Age? _____

Where? _____

"

Funny ☐   Profound ☐   Silly ☐   Bizarre ☐

When was it said? _____ Age? _____

Where? _____

"

Funny ☐   Profound ☐   Silly ☐   Bizarre ☐

When was it said? _____

Where? _____

How would you describe it?

Funny ☐   Profound ☐   Silly ☐   Bizarre ☐

Age? ☐

When was it said? _____ Age? _____

Where? _____

"

Funny ☐   Profound ☐   silly ☐   Bizarre ☐

"

When was it said? _____ Age? _____

Where? _____

"

Funny ☐   Profound ☐   silly ☐   Bizarre ☐

"

When was it said? _____

Where? _____

"

"

How would you describe it?

Funny ☐   Profound ☐   Silly ☐   Bizarre ☐

Age? ☐

☆   ☆

When was it said? _____ Age? _____

Where? _____

"

"

Funny ☐   Profound ☐   Silly ☐   Bizarre ☐

♡   ☆   ♡   ☆   ♡

When was it said? _____ Age? _____

Where? _____

"

"

Funny ☐   Profound ☐   Silly ☐   Bizarre ☐

When was it said? _____

Where? _____

"

"

How would you describe it?

Funny ☐   Profound ☐   Silly ☐   Bizarre ☐

Age? ☐

When was it said? _____ Age? _____

Where? _____

"

Funny ☐ Profound ☐ Silly ☐ Bizarre ☐

"

When was it said? _____ Age? _____

Where? _____

"

Funny ☐ Profound ☐ Silly ☐ Bizarre ☐

"

When was it said? _____

Where? _____

How would you describe it?

Funny ☐   Profound ☐   Silly ☐   Bizarre ☐

Age? ☐

When was it said? _____ ┌─ Age? ─┐

Where? _____

"

Funny ☐   Profound ☐   Silly ☐   Bizarre ☐

When was it said? _____ ┌─ Age? ─┐

Where? _____

"

Funny ☐   Profound ☐   Silly ☐   Bizarre ☐

When was it said? _____

Where? _____

How would you describe it?

Funny ☐   Profound ☐   Silly ☐   Bizarre ☐

Age? _____

When was it said? _____ Age? _____

Where? _____

"

Funny ☐   Profound ☐   Silly ☐   Bizarre ☐

"

When was it said? _____ Age? _____

Where? _____

"

Funny ☐   Profound ☐   Silly ☐   Bizarre ☐

"

When was it said? _____

Where? _____

"

How would you describe it?

Funny ☐ Profound ☐ Silly ☐ Bizarre ☐

Age? ☐

When was it said? _____ Age?

Where? _____

"

Funny ☐   Profound ☐   Silly ☐   Bizarre ☐

"

When was it said? _____ Age?

Where? _____

"

Funny ☐   Profound ☐   Silly ☐   Bizarre ☐

"

When was it said? _____

Where? _____

"

How would you describe it?

Funny ☐   Profound ☐   Silly ☐   Bizarre ☐

Age? ☐

When was it said? _____ Age? _____

Where? _____

"

Funny ☐   Profound ☐   Silly ☐   Bizarre ☐

"

When was it said? _____ Age? _____

Where? _____

"

Funny ☐   Profound ☐   Silly ☐   Bizarre ☐

"

When was it said? _____

Where? _____

99

66

How would you describe it?

Funny ☐ Profound ☐ Silly ☐ Bizarre ☐

Age? ☐

☆ ☆

When was it said? _____ Age? _____

Where? _____

"

Funny ☐ Profound ☐ Silly ☐ Bizarre ☐

"

When was it said? _____ Age? _____

Where? _____

"

Funny ☐ Profound ☐ Silly ☐ Bizarre ☐

"

When was it said? _____

Where? _____

"

"

How would you describe it?

Funny ☐   Profound ☐   Silly ☐   Bizarre ☐

Age? ☐

When was it said? _____ Age? _____

Where? _____

"

Funny ☐ Profound ☐ Silly ☐ Bizarre ☐

♡ ☆ ♡ ☆ ♡

When was it said? _____ Age? _____

Where? _____

"

Funny ☐ Profound ☐ Silly ☐ Bizarre ☐

"

When was it said? _____

Where? _____

How would you describe it?

Funny ☐   Profound ☐   Silly ☐   Bizarre ☐

Age? ☐

When was it said? _____ Age? _____

Where? _____

" "

Funny ☐   Profound ☐   Silly ☐   Bizarre ☐

When was it said? _____ Age? _____

Where? _____

" "

Funny ☐   Profound ☐   Silly ☐   Bizarre ☐

When was it said? _____

Where? _____

"

"

How would you describe it?

Funny ☐ Profound ☐ Silly ☐ Bizarre ☐

Age? ☐

When was it said? _____ Age?

Where? _____

"

Funny ☐   Profound ☐   Silly ☐   Bizarre ☐

When was it said? _____ Age?

Where? _____

"

Funny ☐   Profound ☐   Silly ☐   Bizarre ☐

When was it said? _____

Where? _____

How would you describe it?

Funny ☐ Profound ☐ Silly ☐ Bizarre ☐

Age? _____

When was it said? _____ Age?

Where? _____

"

"

Funny ☐   Profound ☐   Silly ☐   Bizarre ☐

When was it said? _____ Age?

Where? _____

"

"

Funny ☐   Profound ☐   Silly ☐   Bizarre ☐

When was it said? _____

Where? _____

How would you describe it?

Funny ☐   Profound ☐   Silly ☐   Bizarre ☐

Age? ☐

When was it said? _____ Age?

Where? _____

" "

Funny ☐   Profound ☐   Silly ☐   Bizarre ☐

When was it said? _____ Age?

Where? _____

" "

Funny ☐   Profound ☐   Silly ☐   Bizarre ☐

When was it said? _____

Where? _____

How would you describe it?

Funny ☐   Profound ☐   Silly ☐   Bizarre ☐

Age? _____

When was it said? _____ Age? _____

Where? _____

"

Funny ☐ Profound ☐ Silly ☐ Bizarre ☐

When was it said? _____ Age? _____

Where? _____

"

Funny ☐ Profound ☐ Silly ☐ Bizarre ☐

When was it said? _____

Where? _____

How would you describe it?

Funny ☐   Profound ☐   Silly ☐   Bizarre ☐

Age? ☐

When was it said? _____ Age? _____

Where? _____

"

Funny ☐ Profound ☐ Silly ☐ Bizarre ☐

"

When was it said? _____ Age? _____

Where? _____

"

Funny ☐ Profound ☐ Silly ☐ Bizarre ☐

"

When was it said? _____

Where? _____

How would you describe it?

Funny ☐   Profound ☐   Silly ☐   Bizarre ☐

Age? _____

When was it said? _____ Age? _____

Where? _____

"

Funny ☐   Profound ☐   Silly ☐   Bizarre ☐

When was it said? _____ Age? _____

Where? _____

"

Funny ☐   Profound ☐   Silly ☐   Bizarre ☐

When was it said? _____

Where? _____

How would you describe it?

Funny ☐   Profound ☐   Silly ☐   Bizarre ☐

Age? _____

When was it said? _____ Age?

Where? _____

"

Funny ☐   Profound ☐   silly ☐   Bizarre ☐

"

When was it said? _____ Age?

Where? _____

"

Funny ☐   Profound ☐   silly ☐   Bizarre ☐

"

When was it said? _____

Where? _____

How would you describe it?

Funny ☐   Profound ☐   Silly ☐   Bizarre ☐

Age? _____

When was it said? _____ Age? _____

Where? _____

"

"

Funny ☐   Profound ☐   Silly ☐   Bizarre ☐

When was it said? _____ Age? _____

Where? _____

"

"

Funny ☐   Profound ☐   Silly ☐   Bizarre ☐

When was it said? _____

Where? _____

How would you describe it?

Funny ☐   Profound ☐   Silly ☐   Bizarre ☐

Age? ☐

When was it said? _____ Age? _____

Where? _____

"

Funny ☐   Profound ☐   Silly ☐   Bizarre ☐

"

When was it said? _____ Age? _____

Where? _____

"

Funny ☐   Profound ☐   Silly ☐   Bizarre ☐

"

Made in the USA
Middletown, DE
03 February 2018